Praise for
At the End of Myself

"*At the End of Myself* is for every woman who has tried to be perfect and failed. Jackie Quinn has written a book that reminds us of the power we have through Christ when we embrace our weaknesses, defeat the myths of the enemy, and redirect our thoughts, our actions, and our potential into God-honoring purposeful living. This book is filled with practical applications, poignant personal stories, and biblical truth."

>Carol Kent—international speaker and author of
>*When I Lay My Isaac Down* (NavPress)

"The author's transparency is so alluring that you will find yourself living in her world, experiencing her journey and delighting in her triumphs. Jackie Quinn's words are as addicting as her music!"

>J. Otis Ledbetter, PhD—author, conference
>speaker and chairman of the board of the
>Heritage Builders Association

"*At the End of Myself* is not a story of endings but in reality *new beginnings* on the highway to refreshment and authenticity! Jackie Quinn is brave in confronting myths by pressing into the arms of *our loving God*. She says it beautifully,

'God's power is made perfect when our trials are surrendered to Him!' Awesome!"

> Dr. Gary and Barbara Rosberg—nationally known speakers, co-hosts of their nationally syndicated daily radio program, and authors of over a dozen marriage resources

"With warmth and honesty, Jackie Quinn illustrates powerful life lessons learned through both tragedy and triumph. If you are ready to let go and let God take the lead in your life, she has written a book just for you."

> Valorie Burton—life coach, professional speaker, and author of *What's Really Holding You Back?* and *Listen to Your Life*

"In a very practical and meaningful way, Jackie Quinn has effectively shared how faith and trust in God has brought her through life struggles that threatened to damage both her and her family. Her willingness to candidly reveal her personal thoughts and spiritual insight makes her work both inspiring and valuable to those who are seeking to turn their own difficulties into opportunities to learn and grow."

> Loretta Sorensen—freelance writer, speaker, and publisher of *Spirit of the Plains Magazine*, a non-denominational Christian magazine that features personal faith stories from the Northern Plains and surrounding states

AT THE END OF MYSELF
Redefining Strength by Embracing Weakness

by

Jackie Quinn

Copyright © 2007 by Jackie Quinn, Wildflower Ministries

At the End of Myself:
Redefining Strength by Embracing Weakness
by Jackie Quinn

Printed in the United States of America

ISBN-13: 978-1-60034-973-7
ISBN-10: 1-60034-973-0

All rights reserved solely by the author. The author guarantees all contents are original and do not infringe upon the legal rights of any other person or work. No part of this book may be reproduced in any form without the permission of the author. The views expressed in this book are not necessarily those of the publisher.

Unless otherwise indicated, Bible quotations are taken from the Holy Bible, New International Version. Copyright © 1973, 1978, 1984 by International Bible Society. Used by permission of Zondervan Publishing House.

www.xulonpress.com

*to my incredible husband,
whose love and support multiplies my strength
and amplifies my life beyond measure*

CONTENTS

ACKNOWLEDGEMENTS xi

INTRODUCTION xiii

THIS IS NOT FOR YOU TO CARRY
Myth: If those who love me can hurt me, I really don't have anyone else but myself.

Chapter One
  At the End of Myself…I AM DAUGHTER. 19

Chapter Two
  At the End of Myself…I AM WIFE. 29

EBB AND FLOW
Myth: When all I've got is "me," then "me" has to be right.

Chapter Three
  At the End of Myself…I AM SISTER. 39

Chapter Four
  At the End of Myself…I AM FRIEND. 47

ix

MAXIMUM VULNERABILITY
Myth: Those who need help are weak.

Chapter Five
At the End of Myself…I AM MOTHER. 57

Chapter Six
At the End of Myself…I AM MY HUSBAND'S PARTNER. 67

CO-LABORING
Myth: God is so big and powerful; He doesn't have time for me and my problems.

Chapter Seven
At the End of Myself…I AM SINGER. 77

Chapter Eight
At the End of Myself…I AM CHILD OF GOD. 87

WORKS CITED 93

ABOUT THE AUTHOR 95

ACKNOWLEDGEMENTS

Do you ever wonder why one day you're going about your everyday routine, and the next day you have the seemingly far-fetched idea to do something that you've never done before, something that would stretch you to the worn corner of your faded, broken-in blanket that provides boundary to your comfort zone? I know it seems like every one and his or her dog is writing a book these days, whether for publicity or just to be heard. But for me, it wasn't necessarily something I thought I'd ever do, even as a former English major and teacher. In fact, for months I truly tried to shake this call on my life. I tried to tell myself that I haven't lived long enough to have anything of value to offer, that my work doesn't belong on the shelves with the great writers of our time. But the gnawing didn't go away. In fact, chapter ideas began to swirl in my head, and I actually got brave enough to put the words that would shape those chapters down on paper. I've found God works like that, steadily prompting us to follow His lead even when it's not natural to do so.

What follows is the result, but not without much encouragement from the following supportive people in my life…

Alexandria Casey, my editor—This work is better because of your skillful eye and author-to-author advice. Thank you for taking time in the midst of your son's homecoming.

The "Write Stuff" group—my reassurance to call myself "author" and my catalyst for the finish line!

My feedback team and closest friends—for your much-needed input and sincere words of encouragement.

Wildflower Ministries Support Team—for your sustaining belief and prayers.

Mom and Dad—for understanding my story in the midst of yours. Thank you for being big enough to allow me my own walk.

Stacey, Shari, and Justin, my siblings—for being my unwavering and empathetic companions on this life-shaping journey.

Jenna and Kellen, my children—always my inspiration to live fully, to seek and share joy.

Ted, my husband and partner—always the believer in me. Thanks for your undying confidence, unconditional love, and steadfast promise of "no matter what."

Most of all, God—my ever-present comfort and strength. To be in relationship with You is my life's greatest gift and motivation.

INTRODUCTION

When I'm convinced I'm all I need, when I think that one is much better than two, I find myself at "incomplete," and then, I find You.

—"At the End of Myself," Jackie Quinn

I did not consciously live all those years thinking that "I'm it." I embraced myself gradually and unknowingly through the movement of life, clinging to the safety of myself, the safety of my developing talents, the safety of my growing intelligence. You see, I felt that was all I could hold on to in the midst of a chaotic childhood environment.

My parents tried—they really did—to do the best they could by me and my three siblings. Unfortunately, they sometimes got lost in their own pain of their failing marriage and couldn't always see how it was affecting us children. I do not fault them for personally grieving the death of their twenty-five year marriage. But when your parents are not emotionally available for an extended period of time—and during your formative years at that—you turn to whom you know and trust: self.

I turned to myself in a big way over the course of my high school and college years and on into the first years of my marriage and profession. In fact, I became so self-reliant that I lost sight of God's hand in my life. I basically lived by a false coping premise, basing my judgments on and convincing myself of the following:

1) God is so big and powerful; He doesn't have time for me and my problems.
2) If those who love me can hurt me, I really don't have anyone else but myself.
3) When all I've got is "me," then "me" has to be right.
4) Those who need help are weak.

It wasn't until my grade-school-sweetheart-turned-husband Ted and I were in a tragic car accident, that the seeds of change were planted in my heart. Just seven weeks after our wedding, traveling in a severe rain storm, we were spared from the deathly snares of a one-hundred-mile-per-hour impact with a hydroplaning car. I spent my week-long stay in the hospital contemplating why we had lived and the other driver had lost her life. It didn't take long for God to answer: "Jackie, you *must* sing!" I knew the weight that these four words carried…I needed to come to the end of myself…and not just as a singer, but in *all* the roles in my life.

I discreetly tucked this command into the corner of my heart, knowing that when I decided to heed its call, life as I knew it would be over. I didn't warm to that idea well. I was happy being in control. It was safe and predictable. In fact, I held off for a couple more years before my self-reliance rope started to fray at the ends. And finally, when I felt like I couldn't play the game anymore, I relented to life beyond the strength of "just Jackie."

At the End of Myself is about the beauty I have found on the other side of "self." It's about claiming God's "it is *very* good" relationship design (Genesis 1:31). It's about the peaceful discovery of true vulnerability. It's about wanting to share with others the strength in being weak.

THIS IS NOT FOR YOU TO CARRY

Myth: If those who love me can hurt me, I really don't have anyone else but myself.

CHAPTER ONE

At the end of myself...
I AM DAUGHTER.

While standing in front of the open cupboard that kept the fruit cups, I asked my daughter Jenna what she would prefer for lunch "Peaches or mandarin oranges?" In two-year-old fashion, she avoided the question, busily distracted by the small jar of hot fudge syrup on the shelf below. As I asked a second time, she removed the jar from the shelf and began to play "kitchen" with it. Ready to get lunch on the table, I demanded for the third time an answer to my question and that she return the jar to the shelf. As she carried the jar back to the cupboard and placed it on the shelf she said, "Okay, okay, Mom. I want oranges." I impatiently grabbed the cup of oranges and was closing the cupboard behind us as she exclaimed, "Wait! Wait!" At first I was scared I had caught her fingers in the door. I then turned and watched in disbelief as she caught the half-closed door in mid-swing and reached in to perfectly adjust the jar of syrup so that the label would face out. "There," she concluded as she shut the door and walked to the table, satisfied by and proud of her attention to detail. I just stood there, one hand holding the fruit cup, the other keeping my jaw from hitting the floor, and thought, "I'm creating a monster!"

At the End of Myself

Believe it or not, I actually gave up straightening labels and rug fringe about five years ago—three years before having Jenna. Laugh if you will, but outside perfection hides a lot of inside pain. I used this coping mechanism until I was emotionally mature and ready to handle my share (that's right, *my* share) of my parents' divorce. Obviously, however, remnants of my old ways must still surface, as now my daughter is picking up my perfection peculiarities. It's scary to see yourself be so blatantly mirrored! Yet, my Mother mirror (which you'll read about in chapter five) reflects more than meets the eye. It also reflects my thirty-two years as Daughter.

As a child, I was somewhat of a tom-boy, enjoying my days outdoors on the ranch with the animals. I reveled in tree and haystack climbing. I did whatever it took to avoid the kitchen and felt like oil in water behind a sewing machine. I played the ukulele and sang every country song that came over the pick-up's radio while my dad and I bumped slowly through pastures checking cows. I was a passionate, all-or-nothing kind of kid with a deep reservoir of emotion. I wrote my most intense life thoughts and questions in my yellow diary with the bunny rabbit on the cover. At my core I was a fairy-tale romantic, celebrating most the sun-kissed days atop a horse, galloping bareback through the hayfields and section lines dotted with wildflowers.

There's a part of me that would like to look back at my younger years and say I was entirely that happy-go-lucky kid who didn't have a care in the world. But, instead, I carried the weight of the world. I was much too serious about everything. I was a nail-biter and worried miserably about trivial as well as significant things. I was a high-strung, emotional girl who gave my parents fits, especially my mom. I was devastated by anything but A's in school, first place in musical or sports competitions, and purple ribbons in 4-H. I worried if my clothes were right, if every hair had its place, if my laugh sounded weird. I tried to be charming and smart and mature. I longed for approval from my parents, teachers, and coaches, and for friendship with everyone, especially my peers.

Some of this was typical kid stuff—me just sorting out my place in the world. Most of it was me wanting to paste a perfection Band-Aid over all the things that weren't perfect in my life. I believed if I could be and do what everyone wanted, then I could draw attention away from—even forget—the tense undercurrent that engulfed my parents' marriage for the majority of my growing-up years.

Just as Jenna mimics me and my husband, I took my behavior cues from my mom and dad. My mom was an intense mother, expecting the best for and from her four children in every circumstance. Whether she knew it or not, Mom made it clear that she valued perfection. I watched her clean the house until her fingers literally bled. My siblings and I dreaded the "white glove test" she would administer (figuratively speaking) after we completed our weekend cleaning chores. She was the type of mom who felt the need to rip out the crooked stitches in my fifth-grade 4-H sewing project so they would be straight and purple-ribbon worthy when judged at the county fair. She prepared elaborate meals daily and was an active volunteer in our community and church. Though we didn't have much money, she made sure we had what we needed. She pushed us to excel and created opportunities for us to do just that through special athletic and musical instruction. She didn't accept any effort that was what she termed "half-ass."

My dad was just as intense, but in the exact opposite way. His was a silent intensity. He didn't parent us much inside the home, often withdrawing to his recliner for nights of solitary newspaper reading and TV watching. However, when we joined him in his outside world, it was a different story. He was very particular in how we handled the animals, tools, machinery, and vehicles. He made us want to get every first attempt right for fear of his disappointment-rendering silent treatment. Learning to drive a stick-shift, beater pick-up we fondly called "Old Yeller" under his direction was one of the most nerve-wracking things I've ever undergone. Every time I let the clutch go too soon and killed the engine, I worried he thought I was incompetent. He, too, was very intolerant of mistakes and laziness and pushed us to do things right and well. He would say, "If you're gonna do it, do it right" (which I've since heard slip out of my adult mouth on more than one occasion). He, too, was a community leader, serving on school and church boards. He, too, placed high value on perfection.

It's no wonder I became a serious, striving woman who tirelessly labors for perfection in all I do! Although I take responsibility for the extent to which I let my parents' perfection influence shape me, one plus one still equals two. And I've come to find that's not all bad. I'm thankful my parents taught me the value of hard work, how important it is to be conscientious, how not to settle for average. I wouldn't have written this book and have a successful, independent music ministry had I not been raised to know and understand these things. In fact, as a parent now myself, I want to somehow instill the same characteristics in my daughter. However, I have the luxury of hindsight and can discern that there's a fine line between too much and not enough in approaching such goals.

I believe my parents did the best they could with what they had by way of their own experience, knowledge, and resources to raise me and my siblings, especially in the midst of such marital discord. In fact, I often think that if they had put as much energy into their marriage as they did into us kids, it all may have turned out differently.

But it didn't.

I still get sick to my stomach thinking of the night I awoke to hear my mom's uncontrollable sobs and my dad's strained voice in the bedroom next door. I remember trying not to disturb my sister as I left our shared bed and tiptoed to my parents' closed door. I wanted so badly to burst through and make them stop fighting. I thought somehow if they saw me, their elementary-school-aged daughter, they would realize the importance of their bond and their need to keep it together. Instead, I sat in front of the door, arms wrapped around my legs, just rocking back in forth to the rhythm of their destructive, infidelity-implying words. What seemed like an eternity later, I somehow managed to tear myself away and climb back in my bed, knowing that what I had heard marked the end of my little girl's view of marriage.

From then on, I carried the burden. The burden that things weren't what they seemed. The burden that changed my role as Daughter. The burden that I couldn't share with anyone, not even my sisters and brother, not even God.

It affected me deeply to know that my parents' union was not unconditional and genuine. It made me take a cynical view of the world and question everything with sarcasm. I called it "wit" at the time, but it was my way of masking the pain. Remarkably, I still had faith in God, and it did sustain me—as much as I let it. I tried desperately to find my place in the disintegration. I tried to be funny and offer some joy. I tried to protect my siblings to offer some comfort. I tried to be strong for everybody to offer some solace.

Years passed and the coping became old hat. It defined me. In fact, it defined all of us. In and around the volatile emotional outbursts, we all tiptoed by, over, and under the elephant in the room and went on the best we could, mostly focusing on life beyond the walls of our home. It was hard for me, emotionally immature, to draw distinction between Mom and Dad as "married couple" and Mom and Dad as "parents." Anger and distrust seeped into both facets of my relationship with them and gray overcame black and white. Often I was caught in the middle of their manipulation of one another. I teetered back and forth in the blame game, but regularly landed on my dad's side. As psychology goes, I epitomized the "dads and daughters" theory. Even when I knew that there are two sides to every story, I couldn't bear to think of my "hero" as being anything less. It was easier to turn on Mom because she physically removed herself from the situation (for her own important healing and to contribute in providing for our family), leaving us teen-agers to do our own cooking, cleaning, laundry, and growing up while she worked out of town during the week. Ultimately, and at the very core of me, I didn't choose either parent…I chose myself.

Adolescence is all about slowly separating from one's parents and gaining individual autonomy so as to be "self-sufficient" in the real world—that is, able to sufficiently make reasonable judgments and take care of oneself. However, due to the circumstances, I took this development stage even further. At sixteen I became the adult, the parent, the answers when I needed them. I convinced myself that I didn't need anything or anyone. I closed all avenues to vulnerability—it wasn't an option in my finely-tuned survival mode. A chorus I penned in reflection of this time illustrates how I felt:

> *'Cause if you love me, you can hurt me.*
> *Yes, I've been there before.*
> *So I'll keep my heart at an arm's reach*
> *To feel the pain no more.*
>
> —"True Love," Jackie Quinn

That "arm's reach" was many brick walls thick, every year gaining more hardened clay and mortar.

It took me many years after the actual divorce and some good Christian counseling before I could come to a place of understanding and forgiveness toward my parents. I had to do a lot of brick bashing—that is, a lot of healthy boundary-drawing and vulnerable soul-searching to be able to release my pent-up, well-controlled anger and distrust. I had to put a voice to my hurt and let those supportive and close to me in on it. I had to reclaim the happy memories—and there were more than I thought—of my childhood by way of reminiscing and journaling. Most of all, I had to confess my self-reliant cover-up sin to God and come clean about my failure to believe in and trust in Him *one-hundred percent*. I had to make it a priority to co-labor with Him in *all* areas of my life (a concept I'll speak more on in the last section of the book).

I've also had to force myself to not be "perfect" in all things. I quit wearing a watch to avoid being controlled by time and the "perfect" daily schedule. I've made myself keep an eternally unorganized junk drawer. (Actually, at the time of this writing, I've happily realized that more than one junk drawer and cupboard exists in my home.) I now try to allow for spontaneity and fun, instead of resorting to my former calculated, "terminally serious" self. And yes, I most of the time leave the turned-in and turned-sideways labels on canned goods and misaligned fringe on rugs to fend for themselves. Of course, being a mother myself has helped—even forced—the reins to loosen because of just sheer lack of time and energy. It takes a lot of energy to be "perfect," you know!

So what do I want you the reader to take from my thirty-two years as Daughter and apply to your own self-reliance struggle? First, let me tell you what *not* to take. Don't take away from my story a sense of "victim" appeal. That is the last thing I think, or want anyone else to think, of my experience! I can honestly say without reservation that I embrace my past and know I'm in a better place because of it. I'm in a better place because I am closer to my parents now than ever and can give glory to God who brought me out of darkness and into His light. I'm a firm believer in Paul's words: "And we know that in all things God works for the good of those who love him, who have been called according to his purpose" (Romans 8:28). God has made all of this hardship work for good in my life so that I might share His magnificent love and power with others.

What you *can* take is personal responsibility. You perfectionist control mongers know who you are! Be honest with yourself and God. Even though the world would have you believe that self-sufficiency is the only way to success (by the way, even Donald Trump on the hit T.V. show *The Apprentice* needs the advice of two others in the board room before he spits, "You're Fired!"), recognize this prideful trap and its claim on your life. Work to understand how you cope with things you can't control and the effect it has on your life. Work at forgiveness. Most importantly, work at vulnerability and trust. As the Scripture says, "Anyone who trusts in him will never be put to shame" (Romans 10:11).

I can truly say—and the following chapters will continue to attest—that on the other side of "self" there is abundant life! Hopefully my story will lead you on a similarly fulfilling journey.

APPLICATION

Sadly, fifty-percent-plus of all married couples and their families experience separation and divorce after the supposedly sacred "I dos" are spoken. What seems a solution, an ending of sorts, too often creates unending consequences. However, there is hope: CHOICE! Yes, sometimes circumstances are just dealt us, but we are blessed with the free-will card and can choose which hand will we play—that is, how and to what extent we'll react. Matthew 7: 17-20 gives us a measure of evaluation on which to base our choices: *Likewise every good tree bears good fruit, but a bad tree bears bad fruit. A good tree cannot bear bad fruit, and a bad tree cannot bear good fruit. Every tree that does not bear good fruit is cut down and thrown into the fire. Thus, by their fruit you will recognize them.*

SELF-REFLECTION

What does your fruit tree look like? Are your branches brittle or do they reach the sky? Are your leaves spotted or green and lush? Is the fruit you put forth withered and brown or succulent and plentiful? In other words, how have you allowed the painful circumstances in your life to embed and manifest themselves in your behavior and character? What pruning choices could you make to be recognized by God and others as one who "bears good fruit?"

CHAPTER TWO

At the end of myself...
I AM WIFE.

There he was, two seats down from me in the brass section. His polo shirt collar upturned, his nose still brown and freckled from the pool days of summer, his lips imprinted with a red mouthpiece ring from the silver trumpet he was playing. Two years before, he hadn't been very nice to me, the new sixth-grade girl in town. But this year...this year was different. There was a new tension between us. When the trombone player between us leaned over and whispered, "Ted wants to know if you'd be his girlfriend," I felt my heart leap and knew this tension was one from which I didn't want to run. I whispered back, "Yes." And so began "Ted and Jackie."

It's not too often one meets the love of her life in an eighth-grade band class. Ted and I often shake our heads in amazement about the probability, especially now after our eight years of courtship and eleven years of marriage. We truly feel that God set us apart, giving us the security of our relationship during an invariably insecure time in our lives: middle school, high school, and college. Not many can say they had a constantly true friend during those times of change and growth. I know for certain this friendship sustained me over and over again as my parents' marriage slowly dissolved.

The summer Ted and I wed, my parents divorced. Throughout our year-long engagement, the emotional peaks and valleys I went through were incredibly intense. Questions like, "What makes us different? How will we beat the odds?" haunted me. In addition, people around us questioned our youth—only twenty-one years old—in entering into such a huge lifetime commitment. We also heard things like, "You've really never dated anyone else? Are you sure you shouldn't 'play the field' a little?" However, over and over in prayer I kept coming back to a peace about how truly set apart we were, about how God had intended our love to be the special kind that lasts a lifetime. Did we know it wouldn't be perfect? Sure. We had just witnessed first-hand the reality of how tough it could be! But were we willing to see it through regardless? Yes.

It's infamously known that the first year of marriage is the hardest. Not so for us. We had another set-apart challenge with which to contend that actually made marriage seem easy. Seven weeks after we proclaimed "I do!" in front of our family and friends, we found ourselves on separate ambulances headed to the nearest hospital for surgery after a fatal car crash. I remember lying on the emergency room table in excruciating pain, being poked and prodded by various nurses and doctors. They were getting ready to drill into my leg to put my broken femur into traction. Severe whiplash was setting in, and it felt as if glass shards stabbed repeatedly into my head and neck. My many broken ribs made it almost impossible to move or even breathe. And yet in the midst of this extreme physical pain, I shed no tears. All I could do was think about Ted behind the curtain dividing that cold, sterile room. I could hear another team of nurses and doctors working on him. I longed to be with him, to hold him and help him through his pain. I kept insistently asking my mom who was there holding my hand, "How is Ted? Is he okay?" Then, I heard the most haunting sound from behind the curtain. As the nurses removed the shoe that kept his shattered and dislocated ankle intact, I heard from the depths of Ted's being the most agonized, guttural wail. I gripped my mom's hand with all the strength I had left and the tears came... *the kind of tears that come from the deep well within one's helpless soul.*

The next weeks and months of our newly married life together were spent on crutches, waiting for our broken bodies to mend. However, our hearts were open wide and were only beginning to see glimpses of healing. The depth of thought and emotion that comes after the trauma and shock of such an event is indescribable. We mourned for the lost life of the other car's driver. We wondered why it wasn't us. We wondered all the disturbing "what ifs"...What if Ted had died and left me a twenty-one-year-old widow? ...What if I had been paralyzed and he had been taking care of a wheelchair-ridden wife for decades? ...What if... Throughout the next year, I woke many nights to a startled and sweating Ted, bolted out of sleep from the nightmares of slamming on the brakes, yet over and over again crashing into that red Dodge Intrepid.

An event such as this will either shake your faith or make you stronger. Thankfully, the latter was true for us. The reality of how precious life was and how blessed we were to have each other to share each moment with was enough to solidify our young love and bring an instant maturity to our relationship. We thought that if we could get through the emotional burden of this, we could get through anything. Little did we know that our marriage was only beginning to be tested.

Delayed by the car accident's reverberation, the *third* year of marriage was our hardest. We had settled in to the common two-career, two-car, one-house, one-dog life. We were in that "driven" mode of trying to establish a firm foundation for our future. Early mornings and late nights working added up to not much time spent as "Ted and Jackie." What we like to call "marriage maintenance" took a backseat. I've found that when you're not continually focused on something, you revert to "the machine"— that is, whatever comes with as little effort, communication, and thought as possible. In other words, you do what you've always known because it's easy. My machine mode was modeled after my parents' marriage. Failed or not, it's what I knew as "relationship."

As many couples find in their first years of marriage, when two join as one, they bring with them the bags they've carried through life. My bags were loaded with lots of distrust in true, unconditional love. For instance, when Ted said he loved me, I questioned: "Did he really mean it?" I had never seen my parents mean it. I didn't know what that looked like or felt like, and so couldn't truly internalize all that Ted was offering me. Over the years, a wall had been slowly built around my heart that nothing—not even my husband's genuine love—could penetrate. I was so afraid of being hurt and failing at love, that I didn't allow myself to be truly vulnerable.

When I think of the state of my soul at this time, I think of a deep-colored stain on a piece of clothing. The longer it sits there, the more it sinks in and grabs hold of the fibers, spreading its resistant color farther and deeper until no amount of surface rubbing will remove it. I had allowed the distrust and betrayal in my parents' marriage to seep into my own. In fact, I had let it go so far as to transfer all of my anger and distrust from that relationship to my unknowing husband. He didn't know why I questioned him; he just blamed himself and tried harder. Looking back, it still breaks my heart to know how much finger-pointing I did, and that all along, that finger should have pointed directly back at me.

My awakening moment came one afternoon after school had let out early. I had gathered my teaching things and headed out for the twenty-five minute drive home, expecting to get some catch-up things done around the house. When

I made the turn down the block where we lived, immediate fear took my breath away. There was Ted's red Ranger sitting haphazardly in the driveway. He wasn't supposed to be home at this time of day. He should have been coaching basketball practice! I drove slowly down the gravel as I let the instant assumptions develop and spin in my head. By the time I pulled in the drive, I felt a fire pit of anger in my stomach. My body was literally hot and sweating. I rammed the Jeep into "park" and marched into the house, ready to explode in accusations of infidelity. I just knew he, thinking that I wouldn't be home for another hour or so, was in our bed with another woman! I opened the door and walked down the hallway, waiting to hear the sounds of lust that would prove my instincts true.

Nothing. Quiet.

I entered the bedroom to see Ted in our bed…alone. He was huddled under the blankets, his face pale. He heard me come in and rolled over gingerly to face me. He explained that he had come home from work at noon with the flu and had spent the rest of the afternoon vomiting and trying to rest his exhausted body. I hushed him, kissed his clammy cheek, and pulled the covers up over his shoulders. I told him to let me know if he needed anything, then pulled the door closed with trembling fingers. I walked into the next room, pulled a pillow over my face and cried a lifetime's pent-up tears… *the kind of tears that come from the deep well within one's helpless soul.*

How had I come to this place? How had it gotten this bad? Never had I felt so broken. I knew this was my moment of truth. No longer could I go on "handling it," avoiding the issues of my past and allowing them to destroy my present and my future. I had chosen to be in denial and irresponsible with my pain for too long. It was time to *come to the end of myself* and get some help.

After humbly conveying my burdens to Ted, letting him in on years of secret pain, I entered into counseling with a wonderful Christian psychologist. My sweet Ted even agreed to go to some sessions with me to understand further my scope of pain and how it converted to healing in our own relationship. He could have easily thrown his hands up and said, "You deal with it!" But he didn't. Understanding his personal sacrifice in this helped open my eyes to how much he did truly love me. Piece by piece the numbing wall around my heart came down, and I could FEEL again!

My biggest triumph in my many months of counseling was not only drawing closer to Ted, but to God. In all my self-sufficiency, I had pushed Him away just like I had Ted, so that I couldn't feel His true, unconditional love. It was like I was embarrassed that He and Ted would find out that I'm not perfect, that they would know I really wasn't as strong as I had portrayed. The ironic thing is that somewhere in all my Sunday school lessons, I had learned that God was *the all-knowing One* and that I only had the strength I had because *He gave it to me*! Who did I think I was kidding?

The biggest breakthrough came when my counselor asked me to recreate "Jackie" as a young teen, feeling the pain of my parents' divorce. I was to imagine Jesus there with me and the words He might have for me at that moment. Peace softly filled my soul as I put a voice to the words that came to me from Him: "THIS IS NOT FOR YOU TO CARRY." It was then that I understood my healing through His grace and forgiveness. I had a powerful sense of what my role was—and wasn't—in my partnership with God and in my earthly family. I didn't have to "handle it" anymore, for me or for anyone else. Where my strength and ability stopped, God would surely provide ample sustenance. I clasped my hands together in prayer and cried thankful tears... *the kind of tears that come from the deep well within one's "helpless" soul.*

APPLICATION

In the years since God created this good work in us, Ted and I both have now come to know and fully embrace Paul's words to the Corinthians:

> *But He said to me, "My grace is sufficient for you, for my power is made perfect in weakness." Therefore, I will boast all the more gladly about my weaknesses, so that Christ's power may rest on me. That is why, for Christ's sake, I delight in weaknesses, in insults, in hardships, in persecutions, in difficulties. For when I am weak, then I am strong* **(2 Corinthians 12:9-10).**

SELF-REFLECTION

Are you hiding any deep hurts behind a façade of self-sufficiency? Have self-sufficient habits ever prevented you from feeling love and/or accepting help from a spouse or friend? Has your self-reliance isolated you from God's love and power? What steps can you take to become more vulnerable and even "delight in weakness?"

EBB AND FLOW

༃

*Myth: When all I've got is "me,"
then "me" has to be right.*

CHAPTER THREE

At the end of myself...
I AM SISTER.

༄

Jolted from an awful nightmare in which I had to save my best friend Traci from the old woman carrying the gun in her large purse, I awoke to my screaming, bleeding sister sitting up next to me in bed. Shari was holding her nose as blood gushed from the cracks in her fingers onto the pastel bedding below. Through her sobs she screamed to awaken my sleeping parents in the next room, "Moooom! Daaaad! She hit me!" They came running to the rescue and accusingly demanded: "What did you do? Why did you hit your sister?" I tried to explain I didn't punch Shari; I actually swung at the bag lady in my dream who was trying to kill Traci to keep her from getting married. Needless to say, it was a hard sell, since Traci and I were in the fifth grade at the time and nowhere near the getting-married age. Ultimately, the blood gush stopped, the bedding and pajamas were exchanged, and Shari and I were able to sleep again in the same bed...backs to each other, with an imaginary line drawn down the middle, of course.

The whole idea of sharing a bed with your sister is a prime example of what coming to the end of oneself is. First of all, it's often a forced issue. Who would *choose* to share a bed with an older or younger sibling? It certainly wasn't my choice to live out this space-saving scenario from the crib until I was in high school, switching at mid-point from the older to the younger sister! Similarly, it's not often that one *chooses* to let go of "self," at least not without a battle of some kind. I've found that God works like that, for *His* purpose not ours "so the works of God might be displayed" (John 9:3).

Author and minister Max Lucado eloquently describes this in his book It's Not About Me. He says, *"It's not about you....Your faith in the face of suffering cranks up the volume of God's song"* (p. 126). Lucado gives example after example of Biblical and present day people who struggle with struggle and how each is called to showcase God's glory. He explains it this way: *"Your pain has a purpose. Your problems, struggles, heartaches, and hassles cooperate toward one end—the glory of God"* (p. 122).

Secondly, in the sharing of space—a bed or otherwise—young sisters tend to have relational ebb and flow. That is, there are moments when coming to the end of oneself is okay, and there are moments when it's not so easily swallowed, depending on who is the beneficiary. For instance, it's okay to share a room when your older sister is having a slumber party with her friends and your mom tells her she must include you. But, it's not okay when it's your turn to have the slumber party and your younger sister gets to do the same! Or for instance, it's okay—even cool—to be on your older sister's relay team in track, but not okay to every once in a while beat her split times.

These are juvenile but legitimate examples. Notice the selfishness in both the okay and not-okay situations? Either giving or receiving, we want what we want. We want—even compete—to dictate our outcomes. It's hard for us in all of our humanity to bow to the fact that we can't always make these determinations. It's just not our first instinct to accept that others—and God—rely on us to put aside our pride and selfishness and *genuinely* engage in relationship no matter what the outcome. Being a sibling gives us our first practice field for this.

Thankfully, after all of the usual, youthful rivalries, I've discovered as an adult sister the beauty in genuine sibling relationship. How, in all my past history with my two sisters and brother, I can just be *real*. It's not like just meeting someone at church or at the office. You don't have to introduce yourself, explain what you do and why you do it, or hold back your emotion for fear of being judged. All four of us know the others, what the others' passions are, what kinds of food each likes, who reads the book and who watches the movie version. We don't have to explain to each other why an old family story told for the umpteenth time is so funny that it doubles us over and brings tears to our eyes. We don't have to explain why the phone calls between us can be two minutes or two hours long. We don't have to explain the divorce-induced pain we've been through because we've gone through it together. That's genuine relationship.

Be honest. Do you experience God like this? Have you allowed Him to know you in such a real and exposed way? This is the goal, but one that is certainly not reached without forgiveness and grace. It's that ebb and flow thing again, "for all have sinned and fall short of the glory of God" (Romans 3:23). As we struggle with balance between self and God, it's inevitable that we will draw near to God and fall away and draw nearer to Him still. We don't necessarily want to battle, but we do, even if our clinging to self keeps us in a lonely, prideful, unfruitful place.

The apostle Paul describes this struggle like this: "I do not understand what I do. For what I want to do, I do not do, but what I hate, I do" (Romans 7:15). The point is, we can do nothing by our own strength, even if our intentions are good. We need God. We need to need God.

My greatest experience as Sister in which I discovered this soul-quenching need was when I went off to college. Suddenly eight hours from home—eight grueling, car-less hours away from my younger sister and brother—I struggled through sleepless nights in my large, but lonely dorm room, worrying about how I could still buffer for them the rapidly deteriorating family environment. I felt so responsible for their protection from the thickening pain. At a time when I should have been thrilled to be on my own, to have been awarded a vocal scholarship at a prestigious music school, to have the opportunity to pursue the promise of the future and dismiss the dreadful parts of the past, I was grossly consumed by the fact that I wasn't "there" for my siblings, that they were left to face the oncoming divorce alone. I cringed to think that they would go through homecoming football games and proms with the burden of the pretend-everything's-okay family picture, that they would have one less defense against the whispers of our small town gossip. I shouldered this burden so much I let it fog my thinking and squelch any joy I would have in higher learning or in making new friends. Even after being diagnosed as clinically depressed, I retreated to a dark place of denial and blamed the school for my unhappiness, making a transfer at semester time.

Looking back I realize I wanted to be everything for everybody. I wanted to be the strong one. I wanted to take it all away. *I* wanted... In all my wanting I couldn't see what God wanted. How He wanted me to come closer to Him, not farther away in self-reliance. How He wanted me to trust Him. How He wanted me to need Him.

I would like to say that I get it now—at least for the most part. God has demonstrated to me that I'm not a sister savior. And thank goodness I'm not! Can you imagine the enormous responsibility? The endurance one would need? I tried and failed miserably. In fact, it crushed me—and rightly so! There is only one Savior, Jesus Christ, who can handle such burden and make it work for Glory. *The* Savior has *intended* that we are incomplete for the mere fact that it would cause us to need Him.

Dr. Henry Cloud and Dr. John Townsend make this point very clear in their book <u>12 Christian Beliefs That Can Drive You Crazy</u>. They say:

> *"Our needs are designed to draw us closer to God...God doesn't rescue perfect people. He wants people with problems...Those who are poor in spirit, those who are in mourning, those who are meek—those are blessed (Matt. 5:3-5) because they can be filled, can be comforted, can be helped. He never said, 'Blessed are those who have their act together.' If nothing is broken, nothing can be fixed"* (p. 23).

There's life and beauty in needing and being needed. In fact, Cloud and Townsend conclude: *"one of the most spiritual activities you can perform is to need other people"* (p. 18). You see, God not only wants us to need Him to reach our full Christian maturity, but He wants us to need others, intending that we would be "attaining to the whole measure of the fullness of Christ" (Ephesians 4:13).

Do you know that void you feel when it's been too long since you talked—really talked—to your siblings? It's like a piece is missing from the cloth you're cut from. Connection must be made in order to fulfill the innate need God created in you. I rejoice in the days in which I call my older sister, Stacey, to get advice on parenting or business or faith. I need her. I live for the calls when I trade thoughts on love, work, and the future with my younger siblings, Shari and Justin. We share the others' hurts and frustration. We agree and disagree. We swap well-wishes and encouragement. I need each of them. I need to be needed by each of them.

I find it unbelievably ironic that it took a family-destroying act to bring our family together and tighter than ever. Now, that's not necessarily true for all families that endure divorce, but in the case of our family, we are stronger for it. (Not that I would recommend or condone the choice.) I feel that there are too many families out there which just exist, just take for granted the bond they have, the gift of relationship in their midst. Too many families resort to individuality and self-reliance instead of togetherness and compromise. I've witnessed over and over again—from equal-time arguments regarding holiday visits to family inheritance battles—how the need to be right and the need to be in control clouds one's need to need and one's need to be needed.

Needing and being needed by family, particularly siblings, makes for genuine relationships that ultimately uphold the body of Christ and drive us closer to God. By His grace and forgiveness, we can consistently strive to put aside our selfish, relational wants and focus on our God-intended, relational needs to produce genuine, balanced relationships that bring glory to Him and maturity to our faith.

APPLICATION

Call it the middle-child syndrome if you will, but I spent a lot of time in the past trying to be "the strong one" in family matters. Ultimately these efforts left me even weaker emotionally, physically, and spiritually. Thankfully, God has shown me over and over that I'm not a savior, that I can't save my siblings from pain, that each has his or her own path to walk. I've had to find the ebb and flow balance between helping and hindering. I've since claimed Isaiah's words:

> *Do you not know? Have you not heard? The Lord is the everlasting God, the Creator of the ends of the earth. He will not grow tired or weary, and his understanding no one can fathom. He gives strength to the weary and increases the power of the weak. Even youths grow tired and weary, and young men stumble and fall; but those who hope in the Lord will renew their strength. They will soar on wings like eagles; they will run and not grow weary, they will walk and not be faint* **(Isaiah 40: 28-31)**.

SELF-REFLECTION

Have you found yourself trying to be "the strong one" in family matters? Have you ever wanted to help in a family crisis, but found that your efforts were all about the outcome *you* wanted? What would it take to be more discerning of what God wants in these situations? How could you come to know and substitute "hope in the Lord" and "his understanding no one can fathom" for your self-reliant efforts?

APPLICATION

As this whole book magnifies, God is a relational being. As 1 John 4:16 tells us: *God is love*, and love always has an object. Therefore, bearing the image of God, we, too, must be relational; we, too, must be "love." That biblical passage goes on to say, *We love because he first loved us. If anyone says, 'I love God,' yet hates his brother, he is a liar. For anyone who does not love his brother, whom he has seen, cannot love God, whom he has not seen. And he has given us this command: Whoever loves God must also love his brother* (**1 John 4:19-21**).

SELF-REFLECTION

Are you somehow disconnected or estranged from your siblings or other family members? How does this keep you from knowing or coming close to God? How might you embrace your God-intended need to "love your brother" and your need for your brother to love you? How could you communicate this?

CHAPTER FOUR

At the end of myself...
I AM FRIEND.

╼∽╾

It is not ironic at all to me that at the time I sat down to write this particular chapter, I was interrupted by a phone call from my friend Teresa who needed a comforting ear. Now, understanding just how sacred my writing time is (approximately two hours or less—most often less—every other day as determined by my three-year-old's nap time and other office activities), I usually make these calls relatively short. However, hearing the immense sadness in her voice, I dropped everything, closed my laptop to dismiss the blaring blank page, and opened my heart and mind in empathy. For the next forty-five minutes, I listened to her hurts, ached with her, extended what little wisdom I had, and promised I would lift her needs up in prayer.

God works like that through our relationships with others. Just like in our sibling relationships, we're reminded that there's an ebb and flow in our friendships that pushes and pulls us to need and be needed. Even when it doesn't necessarily fit our schedules or our life agenda, God works through others to assure us of what's important: our give and take responsibility to our brothers and sisters in Christ and ultimately to God. "Jesus replied: Love the Lord your God with all your heart and with all your soul and with all your mind. This is the first and greatest commandment. And the second is like it: Love your neighbor as yourself" (Matthew 22:37-39).

My understanding of such a concept didn't always intersect with my friendships. I, like in all my relationships, had it backwards. My giving was actually taking, and my taking was actually giving. In other words, I gave to my friends by actually taking on their burdens as my own, and I took from my friends the chance for them to share my load with me. In turn, I ended up with many unbalanced interactions, with me shouldering too much—and all because I wouldn't allow for true vulnerability and the ebb and flow balance that it brings to a friendship.

A few weeks after Teresa called me, I found myself in great need of an empathetic ear. I was at a breaking point. Already hormonal from being twenty-seven weeks pregnant and stressed from the many looming deadlines from both this book project and my Christmas CD, I received a devastating call from the engineer who recorded my daughter Jenna singing "Away in a Manger." He told me that the data file that held the once-in-a-lifetime take of her little three-year-old voice so magically crooning "the little Lord Jesus lay down His sweet head" had been corrupted. On top of this, I had just received word that I didn't pass my glucose screening test and would have to test again for gestational diabetes. Needless to say, it was a very stressful time.

The old Jackie would have forged ahead through all of this turmoil without letting on how heavy her load was. But embracing that relational ebb and flow concept and knowing that God works through His people, I was able to answer *honestly* when Teresa happened to bump into me on the street and ask, "How *are* you?" Through welling tears, I shared my plight, and she listened to my hurts, ached with me, extended what wisdom she had, and promised she would lift my needs up in prayer. The old Jackie wouldn't have understood the strength I gained in that moment from my sister in Christ.

Ecclesiastes 3:1 reminds us: "There is a time for everything, and a season for every activity under heaven." When I recount my friendship seasons, I'm first taken back to when I was a senior in high school. I was voted Miss Congeniality in two different pageants. These titles were more important to me than the First Runner Up titles I attained in the same pageants. I really did strive to be friends with everyone, and not just for the win, but for the genuine cause of relationship. I enjoyed my classmates and the many friends I had outside of my hometown. Even into college and my first "real world" years, I was told I was "a good friend," a "good listener" and that I offered "good advice." Many people called upon me to help them through their problems. And that's exactly what I did...so I didn't have to focus on my own.

The next friendship season I experienced was more about filling a companionship void in my life. As a young coach's wife, I had a choice: spend a lot of time by myself moping that my husband was away all of the time working, or reach out to my friends to fill that screaming need for camaraderie. I had lots of lunch and movie dates with girlfriends and played on a city volleyball league, but still found myself spending more time "saving" everyone else in their crises than letting people into mine.

Looking back, I would have died had any of my friends known the personal struggles I've included in this book! I thought that if they knew my own weaknesses, they would think I was less qualified as a friend, as a listener, as an advice giver. What I've found is that my life experiences, my joys and struggles, have actually made me *more* qualified to reach out...and also reach in.

I've now attained the season of friendship where I can be in the "need" seat as well as the "needed" seat. In fact, this describes well my closest friendships. They're the kind of friendships that have allowed me the ebb and flow dynamic. They've offered me a time to need and a time to be needed, a time to grow and a time to stand still, "a time to weep and a time to laugh, a time to mourn and a time to dance" (Ecclesiastes 3:4). They've allowed me to move away, but stay close. They've left room for me to get busy with my own life, but then plug in to theirs when I can. For this I am extremely grateful and count myself blessed beyond measure.

In Ecclesiastes chapter four we're told: "Two are better than one, because they have a good return for their work: If one falls down, his friend can help him up. But pity the man who falls and has no one to help him up!" (vs. 9-10). In the past, I wouldn't allow anyone to help me up after falling, or even extend a hand in mid-fall. Once I was able to see that I needed to need the people that God so intricately placed in my life, I realized the rest of the author's truth: "Though one may be overpowered, two can defend themselves. A cord of three strands is not quickly broken" (vs. 12).

I often think of this strength-in-numbers concept when I reminisce about my former days as Music Teacher. I was responsible for showcasing the talents of approximately three hundred students in the annual Christmas Program. Of course, being the ambitious first-year teacher I was, I took it upon myself to literally recreate Bethlehem's live nativity setting at Sacred Heart School. Envision, if you will, about twenty-five second-graders clamoring up the steps of the city courthouse in bathrobes to reenact the Caesar census scene. Imagine an eighth-grade Mary wrapped in a blue sheet on an actual donkey being led by an eighth-grade Joseph (who kept losing his brown-blanket wrap to the hooves of the clumsy beast). Picture several unruly lambs in the barn running around an actual babe in the manger and the rest of the city-slicker class looking on, dressed in wisemen, shepherd, and angel garb. Quite a sight, let me tell you! Aside from the elementary awkwardness, however, beautifully touching moments were achieved. And certainly not by me alone!

I came to realize the success of such a seemingly impossible feat was achieved only by teamwork. I needed to call upon many talented, resourceful people to pull such an undertaking off, many of whom were my colleagues and friends. Had I claimed the overused mantra "If I want it done well, I'll just do it myself" and attempted to design the costumes, herd the animals, run the video camera, *and* direct the music, the whole program would have gone awry—and at the emotional expense of three hundred elementary kids! Even though it was hard—okay, extremely difficult—for me to admit that I couldn't do it all on my own, I recognized that the program was much more successful with many involved than if it was dependent on me and my skills alone.

Another example of when I came to know the power in yielding to friendship was when my ministry development company assigned me the task of creating a ministry support team. Every proud, self-reliant fiber in my body fought this assignment. It was so difficult—okay, excruciating—to go to those closest to me and ask for help in building a sound financial and prayer foundation for my ministry. I choked and held back tears with every living room meeting I held. I shared with people my life's call, my hopes and dreams to use my gifts to make an impact in ministry. I asked them to believe in me, even in the unknowns. Talk about vulnerability! I really had to step outside of myself in faith, because the Jackie who had normally only let people get within an arm's reach of her heart just couldn't go there. God's third stabilizing strand in the cord was the only thing that got me through that faith-stretching process.

The result is truly "a cord of three strands not quickly broken," as I'm now lifted up each month by hundreds of supporters whom I consider dear friends. The gift this is to me is not measured by the monetary donations nor the number of prayers prayed, but by the mere fact that I'm reminded this ministry is much bigger than me. There is power and beauty in that beyond comprehension.

Proverbs 27:17 tells us: "As iron sharpens iron, so one man sharpens another." God can and does work through His people. Friendship and teamwork provides an avenue in which His strength can come through and complement us right where we're at, in all the seasons of our lives. If we allow ourselves to be vulnerable enough to experience the friendship/team effect, we will reap many life-giving rewards.

A Word of Caution: Just as I share how good friendship can be at the end of ourselves, I'd also like to throw in a small warning here and make a distinction between naivety and discretion. Unfortunately, there are lost people out there who could and sometimes do deliberately pull us down. We've heard the saying: "You are who you hang out with." We warn teenagers about this, hoping they don't fall into the "wrong crowd." But we need to take care as adults as well to protect our vulnerability. Yes, even though it sounds contradictory, I said "protect our vulnerability." In all my promotion of vulnerability and trust in this book, I'm also ever-mindful of those who walk this earth with a "what's in it for me?" attitude, those with total disregard for their responsibility in a *balanced* relationship. I encourage you to surround yourself with those who will truly be the "iron that sharpens iron" (Proverbs 27:17) in your life and not those who will manipulate your vulnerability and trust with their own best interests in mind. That is not true friendship and shouldn't be mistaken as such.

APPLICATION

Throughout life we experience many seasons. No matter what, we can rejoice that *He has made everything beautiful in its time* (Ecclesiastes 3:11).

SELF-REFLECTION

How would you describe your current season of friendship? How would you rate the balance you feel between the "need" and "needed" roles you play as Friend? How might you allow God, in His perfect timing, to transform this into a "beautiful" balance?

APPLICATION

As mentioned in this chapter, *Proverbs 27:17* tells us: *As iron sharpens iron, so one man sharpens another.* I believe it's an imperative focus in friendship.

SELF-REFLECTION

Who of your friends has your best interests in mind and makes you better? Likewise, who do you "sharpen" in friendship? How could you improve this outreach? Which of your friendships leaves you feeling dull and perhaps used? How could you convey and perhaps remedy this?

MAXIMUM VULNERABILITY

∽

Myth: Those who need help are weak.

CHAPTER FIVE

At the end of myself…
I AM MOTHER.

∽

I recall the moment right after laboring to deliver my first child, my daughter Jenna. Ted, with mixed emotions as the devoted husband and the new dad, went with the attending nurses to weigh and measure her crimson red, wrinkly body. One nurse remained and tended to me as my body shook and recovered from the trauma of birth. She asked, "How do you feel?" I couldn't wipe the smile of satisfaction and delight off of my face as I responded, "I just want to shout, 'I AM WOMAN!'" She laughed and shook her head in understanding. All of those days of worrying if my hair was just right, or my hips looked too big in that pair of jeans, or if my in-laws would approve…it all went away with Jenna's first beautiful cry. I finally knew what I was physically and mentally capable of and had nothing more to prove. Or so I thought.

A mentor and friend of mine in the music business once told me she had gotten to such a successful place in her life in which she felt she had mastered all the skills needed to do her job, that she decided to buy a string bass and take lessons just to be bad at something, just to feel like a novice again, just to keep her pride in check. I laughed at this, because I knew it would probably be less than a month and she would have that particular skill mastered as well; it was just her style. But I also marveled at the risk she took to put herself in such a place of vulnerability. How many of us willingly try something we're bad at? Don't we usually stick to the things we can do well and take pride in? With this in mind, why would anyone ever decide to have a child? Sure, anyone can be a parent, but there's no guarantee of success or mastery no matter how great your skill or your commitment. Even in light of that first confident moment in the birthing room (and a few pats on the back thereafter), I have discovered that parenting will be my eternally unconquered string bass.

Motherhood strikes every chord of vulnerability in my being, with no amount of mastery in sight. It affects my every mood, my every thought, my every sleeping and waking moment. Jenna can bring to the surface every emotion I'm capable of...from worry that I'm messing her up, that I'm not doing enough, that I'm doing too much...to being so upset one minute at her dinner-table disobedience...to laughing so hard the next minute at her goofy response which prompts me to leave the room and salvage any amount of parental authority and dignity I have left...to crying tears of joy when her three-year-old voice speaks her delicate bedtime prayers. And that's just the surface!

Unless you've experienced it, it's almost too difficult to describe the beautifully consuming nature of what it is to be a mom. In fact, I had originally thought I'd title this chapter *I AM PARENT* so as not to exclude the men who may be reading. However (and I'm sure many men would probably agree), there's just something indescribably anointed and unique about motherhood. To discover the miracle of life growing inside one's body—never had I personally undergone such transformation of heart, such relinquishing of control! Oh, I was like millions of women before me, who *thought* they could control the whole process. I read the books, ate right, exercised, decorated the nursery just so, planned to have the perfect angel of a child. Yet there were two distinct moments early on in which I felt that the whole having-a-baby thing had very little to do with me, that I was profoundly *at the end of myself.*

~ ~ ~ ~ ~

The first defining moment occurred after preparing for the clinical visit in which my husband and I would have to say "yes" or "no" to an AFP test (alpha-fetoprotein, also called Trisomy 21). The AFP test is a blood test that is used to assess the likelihood that a pregnant woman is carrying a child with a neural tube defect or Down syndrome. The mere concept of such a test is quite a catalyst for serious discussion among couples, whether a negative test result would spur a decision for pregnancy termination or not. It made us start thinking of possibilities that hadn't occurred to us in all of the initial dreaminess of being new parents.

Up until this moment, I had been caught up in the whole miracle and, of course, the baby's gender mystery and the common question posed by the curious: "What are you having, a girl or a boy?" I have to admit I fell prey to the common—and safe—reciprocal response: "We don't care as long as he or she is healthy and has all twenty fingers and toes." After stopping to consider what it would mean if he or she didn't have the "correct" number of appendages, if he or she would be born handicapped, I realized my lack of control in it all...and my lack of faith. Who was I to think that book reading or nursery decorating or hoping for perfection would make everything okay? And what made me think that my definition of "healthy" was by God's standards? Was not every child of His creation? Talk about your *at-the-end-of-myself* epiphany! We declined the test, and I distinctly remember getting on my knees and praying fervently to God through my tears:

Dear Father,

Please forgive my pride, my narrow-mindedness, and my lack of faith. I know that You have your hand on this whole pregnancy and that You will protect my baby from any physical or mental handicaps if it is Your will. I do not take lightly the responsibility I have as this baby's parent, but please make known to me where I stop and where You start. Please give Ted and me the courage to face whatever You intend for us and the peace and reassurance that You will be near us and guide us through it all. We praise You for this mystery and blessing in our lives! Thank you for giving us this chance to grow closer to You. Amen.

The next time I was asked if I was having a boy or girl, I answered whole-heartedly: "We will love whatever God intends!"

~ ~ ~ ~ ~

The second major control-relinquishing moment I experienced as a mom was just weeks after I had Jenna. I had trouble sleeping every night, even between feedings. I couldn't shake the fear I felt about leaving her to her dark bedroom in her large crib all by herself. I would toss and turn at any movement that crackled over the baby monitor, or even at the silences that lasted too long. I would listen for any change in her breathing patterns, ready to run down the stairs to rescue her from a blanket around her neck or over her head. When I did fall into sacred sleep, I would eventually bolt straight up, sweating and frantically rummaging through my bed blankets trying to find Jenna, fearful I had fallen asleep while nursing her and had left her to be smothered. (Ironically, I had never attempted to nurse her while lying in my bed because I was so fearful of such a thing!) After several nights of this fitful panic, I hit my breaking point.

Still in a spell of sleep and thinking I had heard Jenna crying inconsolably, I tore the bed apart looking for her, screaming her precious name. I hysterically got up to run throughout the house searching for her, shrieking, "Where is she? I can't find her!" Ted finally grabbed me and held me tight, saying, "She's okay, Jackie. She's sound asleep in her crib. There's nothing to worry about. Everything's alright." I fell into his arms and sobbed. I'd never known such an overtaking fear as this. I went to her bedside and lightly brushed her soft, dark hair and stroked her little cheek with my trembling fingers. The light of the moon shining in the window revealed the rise and fall of her restful breaths. I let out a heavy sigh and felt God's comforting presence come over me. In that moment I realized she was not mine first. She was God's child first...and I, only her caretaker. When I couldn't be with her, He was with her. When I couldn't sustain her, He would. He was her protector, her comfort, her peace. Again I prayed through my cleansing, relinquishing tears...

Dear Father,

I give her to You. Please soothe my fears, for I trust You and know You will protect her from harm and from my shortcomings. Thank you for blessing me as Jenna's mom on this earth and showing me through this moment my place in the picture. Rid me of my anxiety and give me the wisdom to raise her in the way she should go. Amen.

By the grace of God, I slept like a baby the rest of that night.

~ ~ ~ ~ ~

That's not to say that I have carried peace in my motherly heart every moment thereafter. But I have learned to take my anxiety and fears to the One who entrusted me with this great responsibility in the first place. I have vowed over and over to be God's partner in parenting and not try to do it all by myself. Stormie Omartian speaks profoundly of this concept in her book <u>The Power of a Praying Parent.</u> She says:

> *We don't want to limit what God can do in our children by clutching them to ourselves and trying to parent them alone. If we're not positive that God is in control of our children's lives, we'll be ruled by fear. And the only way to be sure that God* **is** *in control is to surrender our hold and allow Him full access to their lives. The way to do that is to live according to His Word and His ways and pray to Him about everything.* (p. 33)

Hmmm...pray about everything. You can say that again! Deciding to be a mom—and a stay-at-home one at that—has kept me on my knees A LOT! I have said over and over to Ted: "Put me in the male-dominated, cut-throat, corporate world and I could do it; it would be hard, but I could do it. But put me in charge of a dependent child, directing everything from bowel movements to brain development—and not just for eight or ten hours, but twenty-four hours a day, seven days a week—and see me stretched to my limit!" This role in my life is the epitome of *at the end of myself.* It's complete and utter sacrifice. It's the ultimate joy and hardship. Omartian puts parenting this way:

It's the best of jobs. It's the most difficult of jobs. It can bring you the greatest joy. It can cause the greatest pain. There is nothing as fulfilling and exhilarating. There's nothing so depleting and exhausting. No area of your life can make you feel more like a success when everything is going well. No area of your life can make you feel more like a failure when things go wrong. (The Power of a Praying Parent, p. 13)

Yet, even in all its paradox, being "Mama" is the most rewarding, most beautiful thing I could have ever chosen to do. Nothing else could truly show me what I am and what I'm not. Nothing else could bring me as close to God, witnessing His work and feeling His presence every day through the little blessing I call "Jenna." Nothing else so challenges my faith and calls me to be as Christ-like.

I could offer example after example of how coming to the end of oneself as "Mother" is the *ultimate* celebration of strength through vulnerability and weakness. For those who risk and relinquish control in this way, a fuller and more soul-satisfying life awaits—but only by tremendous dependency on God, the first and best parent of all.

APPLICATION

One of the most called upon Bible verses on parenting is Proverbs 22:6 stating, ***Train a child in the way he should go, and when he is old he will not turn from it.*** Many parents place the emphasis on the "should" and take this to mean that the proper early training will result in a God-fearing, commandment-following adult. In other words: good parents will raise good children. However, what if the verse is read "Train a child in the way **he** should go…" with an emphasis on the fact that we are each uniquely created and therefore, there is a distinct path for us as parents to nurture accordingly for each of our children? Either way it creates a high parental standard to live up to…that is, if we choose to do it alone.

SELF-REFLECTION

Do you feel pressured by "shoulds" as a parent? How often do you take your parental pressures, concerns, and fears to God in prayer? What steps could you take to fully trust and depend on God for wisdom and guidance in these areas?

APPLICATION

Through all the second-guessing and weariness of motherhood, I've often placed myself at Jesus' feet as he told His disciples:

> **Blessed are the poor in spirit,**
> **for theirs is the kingdom of heaven.**
> **Blessed are those who mourn,**
> **for they will be comforted.**
> **Blessed are the meek,**
> **for they will inherit the earth.**
> **Blessed are those who hunger and thirst**
> **for righteousness,**
> **for they will be filled.**

Blessed are the merciful,
>   for they will be shown mercy.
Blessed are the pure in heart,
>   for they will see God.
Blessed are the peacemakers,
>   for they will be called sons of God.
Blessed are those who are persecuted
>   because of righteousness,
>   for theirs is the kingdom of heaven
(Matthew 5:3-10).

SELF-REFLECTION

As a parent, do you feel a need to be independent and do things perfectly? How often do you find yourself "poor in spirit" or "hungry and thirsty" as a parental disciple? How might you invite God to carry your parental burdens? How might you, as a mom or a dad, internalize the promises He makes in the Beatitude verses above?

Chapter Six

At the end of myself...
I AM MY HUSBAND'S PARTNER.

❦

I know a woman whose husband, after thirty-some years of marriage, has never seen her without her makeup on, except by the moonlight in their bedroom. At night she waits until he's already in bed before she comes into the room with a freshly washed face, and in the morning, she's up before him to reapply in the secrecy of the bathroom. I know another woman who after twenty-some years of marriage won't undress in front of or have intimate relations with her husband unless the lights are off, and it's completely dark. Surprising? Maybe. But more common than you think.

Knowing this, I would love to travel all over the world and gather all the twenty-something young women to my soap box. I would look into each vibrant, yet yearning face and say, "It's really okay. You're enough."

I would speak from my own experience, sharing with them how spending hours in front of a mirror to make each unruly hair "just right" is not worth the frustration, because most likely any compliments that come their way would be deflected by their own self-disbelief. I would share with each of them how putting up a hard-core, assertive front and being the independent, domineering woman society would have them believe they should be will leave them empty and continually seeking. I would share with them what author Stasi Eldredge in her book Captivating puts so eloquently: *"A woman in her glory, a woman of beauty, is a woman who is not striving to become beautiful or worthy or enough. She knows in her quiet center where God dwells that he finds her beautiful, has deemed her worthy, and in him, she is enough."* (pp. 134-135)

It's taken me the course of my eleven years of marriage and the birth of my first child to begin to break down the mixed women's lib messages that have been so deeply ingrained by society, by all the striving women who've gone before. Sure, our mothers and grandmothers wanted more for us. "Don't ever settle," many of them would say. But I don't believe they would have chosen for us the unending emptiness we find through independent and self-reliant pursuits. I think they would have wished for us young women a balance—a way that would include our own unique identities and gifts *within relationship* without such struggle for happiness and self-assuredness. That way begins with Peter's words: "Your beauty should not come from outward adornment, such as braided hair and the wearing of gold jewelry and fine clothes. Instead it should be that of your inner self, the unfading beauty of a gentle and quiet spirit, which is of great worth in God's sight" (1 Peter 3: 3-4).

My young daughter gets this. I watch her three-year-old frame as she twirls in front of the full-length mirror in her hand-me-down, but beautifully flowing gown. Her too-big sparkling plastic shoes make the turns cumbersome, and the hot pink and purple beads swish and tangle around her neck, but she doesn't seem to mind. The shy smile and hazel shimmer to her eyes that start slowly but soon transform her face say it all: "I feel special!"

Jenna innocently claims that set-apart feeling as she walks the room curtsying as if Cinderella. Unlike we adults, she doesn't speculate if she's worthy or enough. She just embraces the truth: that there is no other like her, that God has uniquely designed her and has chosen her to emulate Him in the way that only Jenna can.

Do you ever ask yourself what happens in the passage of time between our play clothes and our adult attire? What shoves our self-esteem back into the under-the-bed trunk and permits only occasional peeks at what could be—what's meant to be? What makes us feel unworthy of our spouse's love, or a promotion at work, or a simple compliment about our beautiful flower garden or our yummy apple pie? What would happen if we instead twirled in delight to the rhythm of God's promise: "I am fearfully and wonderfully made" (Psalm 139:14)?

It's a wonder to know that "all the days ordained for me were written in Your book before one of them came to be" or that God's thoughts about us "outnumber the grains of sand" (Psalm 139:16-18). How then, can we not count ourselves special or enough? It's a hard concept to grasp and internalize. We question like King David: "When I consider Your heavens, the work of Your fingers, the moon and the stars, which You have set in place, what is man that You are mindful of him?" (Psalm 8: 3-4).

I fall in this trap too. I question myself as I speak, write, or sing, wondering what in the world little ol' me has to offer. I wonder what, after eleven years, keeps my husband full of love for me. I wonder why God would deem me worthy of a beautiful daughter and the son in my womb. And as I look out at my audiences when I present, I see the same questions and doubt. From the soon-to-be-divorced husband, to the weary mom, to the apprehensive middle school student, to the weathered prison inmate, I see much uncertainty in self-worth.

A song that I've come to include in my music ministry programs is "Who Am I?" by Casting Crowns. It speaks powerfully to the truth that Jenna knows and has not yet come to question: that we are worthy regardless of our faults. Not just because God thought enough of us to make a distinct blue-print with our individual names (as if that wouldn't be enough), but because He sent Jesus to wipe away all of our doubt and uncertainty so that we could be free to claim such abundance! The chorus says it well:

> *Not because of who I am, but because of what You've done.*
> *Not because of what I've done, but because of who You are.*
> *I am a flower quickly fading, here today and gone tomorrow,*
> *A wave tossed in the ocean, a vapor in the wind.*
> *Still You hear me when I'm calling.*
> *Lord you catch me when I'm falling,*
> *And You've told me who I am: I AM YOURS.*

So what does feeling beautiful or worthy or enough have to do with being my husband's partner? Everything! When I as a woman and a wife realized that I no longer had to strive to prove my worth, no longer had to hide my imperfections — that was the day I truly became my husband's partner.

You see, in all the striving and hiding, I was keeping something from Ted. In essence I was saying, "You can have this much of me, but I'm holding back the rest for myself to avoid failure and rejection." In other words, I prevented true vulnerability in my relationship with him.

At the brink of maximum vulnerability, most of us shut down. It's an uncomfortable place to be. It makes us squirm to know that someone might find us out, that the outside does not reveal the inside.

Well-known talk show host Oprah Winfrey ran a story series called the "Debt Diet." She featured couples who were in extreme debt and encouraged them by way of counselors and other resources to become debt free. It amazed me to see just how blatantly and just how many couples kept their dirty laundry debt issues from each other. They would explain it away by saying, "My husband would just die if he knew…" or "I couldn't possibly tell her…." Letting each other in on such dark secrets would mean maximum vulnerability, and many just choose not to go there.

In chapter two I revealed that as a younger wife I chose not to "go there" with Ted. I didn't want him to know that the outside didn't match the inside. I wanted to be Super Wife and have it all together: I could handle the pain of my parents' divorce by myself, all the while contributing to society by my life's work, and meticulously cooking and cleaning for him with my toe nails painted and my ideal weight balancing the scale. But what I found is that if I can't be me, then he can't be him.

When I manipulate the puzzle, when I tweak the edges just so, I rob Ted of his individual ability to put the pieces together. He can't reveal himself to me, offering his full compassion to me, if I keep things from him. If I can't trust him with my deepest fears, frustrations, and failures, how will he get the chance to be trustworthy? How can we truly fulfill God's command to "join as one" if I continue to independently cling to "two" and separate us by what I decide to reveal and not reveal (Matthew 19:5)?

Oh, the beauty in barriers-down true love! By far, I wouldn't say I've mastered it. But I have tasted it, and it is good. In fact, like God's proclamation after creating man and woman, "it is *very* good!" (Genesis 1:31; italics mine). It is *very* good to spend the energy I would have normally put toward hiding and use it to just concentrate on being me. It is *very* good to be partners with the man who complements me and all my strengths and shortcomings. It is *very* good to know that this is what God intended for me.

As I mentioned in chapter three, it might come as a huge surprise to some, but our Creator God intended for us to be incomplete. That's right! He knew exactly what He was doing when He left a huge void in each of our hearts. He knew that by leaving us incomplete, He was creating a drive within us to seek what it is that would fill us. As I said before, many of us, especially young women, go about our days just striving and seeking, trying new and different approaches to fill the void. We turn to work, money, food, beauty remedies, extreme exercise, so-so relationships, or alcohol and drugs, grasping at anything that brings even short-lived contentment. But our Creator gave us a sustaining contentment: Himself. We can know and be filled by Him through study and prayer, and we can know and be filled by Him through His people. I draw closer to God when I draw closer to my husband in partnership. It's a lights-on, makeup-off type of vulnerability worth more than any independent, self-reliant pursuit!

APPLICATION

Of all the striving we do, the most fulfilling and rewarding is drawing closer to God. The apostle Paul tells us: *Do you not know that in a race all the runners run, but only one gets the prize? Run in such a way as to get the prize. Everyone who competes in the games goes into strict training. They do it to get a crown that will last forever* (**1 Corinthians 9: 24-25**).

SELF-REFLECTION

How might you find the balance between the "running" Paul speaks of and the "quiet center" Stasi Eldredge speaks of? What kind of "strict training" would be necessary to achieve this? How might this amplify your relationships, especially your marriage partnership? How might this amplify your life?

APPLICATION

Ted and I rejoice that after declaring the first five days of creation as: *It is good*, God then created the set-apart relationship design of man and woman and proclaimed: *It is very good!* (**Genesis 1**). He went on to declare: *It is not good for the man to be alone. I will make a helper suitable for him* (**Genesis 2:18**).

SELF-REFLECTION

Do you feel alone in your relationships? What would it take for you to feel the depth of God's intended *"very* good" sentiment? How could you risk maximum vulnerability and be a "helper suitable" in relationship? Likewise, how could someone be a "helper suitable" to you? How could you communicate this?

CO-LABORING

*Myth: God is so big and powerful;
He doesn't have time for me and my problems.*

CHAPTER SEVEN

At the end of myself...
I AM SINGER.

❦

Orphan Annie got me a trip to Disney Land. Shirley Temple got me a second place finish at the local Snow Queen Contest and a yummy, striped lollipop bigger than my second-grade face. Dolly Parton (okay, maybe her exaggerated and replicated physique) got me lots of laughs in the local summer parade. Each personality gave me a way to showcase my budding vocal talent and entertainer qualities at a very young age. Can you imagine what would have happened had *American Idol* or *Nashville Star* been a thing back then? I probably would have been right in there with all the star-struck wanna-bes. Thankfully, God protected me from that walk and somehow—certainly not because I made it easy—kept me on or near the path He marked just for me.

Some would say mine must have been an easy walk with such a distinct gift. I would beg to differ. I picture myself, an eight-year-old on the South Dakota Miss Teen Pageant stage. I, as South Dakota's named Annie-Look-Alike, was the special entertainment that evening with my Annie head of red (okay, auburn, but real) curls, and my home-made, but look-alike red dress and shiny, black patent shoes. I sat on a stool in the middle of the spotlighted stage and strummed my not-at-all-like-Annie ukulele and belted out a less-than-pageant-appropriate selection, "Crawdad Hole." Right after this unrefined folk tune, I stood to be interviewed by the pageant's prominent Master of Ceremonies. After meekly answering his questions (I wasn't so keen on speaking in public, just singing), I was asked to sing another. I agreed and instinctively went to lower myself back on the stool provided. Before I knew it, I found myself planted hard on the stage floor. Without me knowing, some stage hand had taken the stool away while I was doing my interview! I was horrified, to say the least, but somehow regained my composure enough to summon another song, although I don't even remember what I sang. My fingers and lips were on automatic, and the insecure part of me—that part that worried I had the audience's pity and not their admiration—just couldn't wait to sink deep into my seat in the sea of dark faces just on the rim of the spotlight's burn.

Throughout the years I've had moment after moment like this in which I'm caught between yearning to stand out and wanting so much to hide. Knowing me now, a singer and speaker in front of thousands annually, one might not believe that. But there were times, when I was much younger and immature, that I just didn't want to have the gift God gave me, or if I did, I wanted to be in control of it, not relinquish it to Him or anyone else!

Those times mostly came when my singing talent set me apart from my peers and my siblings. If you understand basic pre-teen and teen psychology at all (I spent five years as a middle school teacher and so am very acquainted with it), you know that it's hard to be good at something when those in your age group aren't. It places you under a huge, scrutinizing microscope or holds the measuring stick even higher than normal. It makes you subject to a jealous "mean and nasty" instead of a respectful "encouraged and supported." For instance, in front of my middle school peers, I didn't want to let on what I could do, and so sang quieter in music class than I would have at home in my bedroom. I didn't want to draw attention and be thought of as different—and certainly not better—especially since I was the new kid in town. Later, when all of my high school friends sang boldly to all the tunes that came over their booming car stereos during our road trips, I just sat quietly and listened. It's as if I was able to turn on and off the musical faucet and direct the flow of my gift as I saw best suited me and my circumstances.

In my sibling relationships my talent was an issue we never really discussed, but was always very present and usually just under the surface of most of our interactions. My two sisters and brother knew very well my label "the singer" in the family. I think they thought that made me the favorite because I was in the public eye more and hence received more public acknowledgement. It was hard for me to deal with this because, again, part of me just wanted to be the second of the four Scott kids. But frankly, part of me really enjoyed the attention I received from doing something I deep-down really loved.

In lesser forms, this blessing-versus-burden barrier of sorts even carried over into my adult world. Even now after I get done with a performance, some of my closest friends and family still don't know how to handle a "good job" comment or any kind of comment for that matter. Not that I need to hear it because I'm now very comfortable in my own skin and I know my place in God's work, but I often feel that squirming tension and can tell they want to say it, and for some reason it's too awkward to comment on the thing that they perceive sets us apart. Silly, but true. And sadly, for this very reason, many gifted people—children and adults—leave their sacred abilities by the wayside for fear of standing out and being treated differently.

Not willing to ignore my gift and understanding more God's call on my life, my adult answer to this peculiar behavior is: "Singing is just what *I* do. Everyone, by God's design, has their thing. Singing just happens to be mine."

Author Max Lucado explains this in his book <u>Cure for the Common Life: Living in Your Sweet Spot</u>: "*Look at you. Your uncanny ease with numbers. Your quenchless curiosity about chemistry. Others stare at blueprints and yawn; you read them and drool. 'I was made to do this,' you say. Heed that inner music. No one else hears it the way you do*" (p.2).

In my family alone this concept is evident. My older sister is a Business Administration and Political Science major turned Mary Kay Sales Director and part-time Loan Originator. My younger sister is an Athletic Trainer major turned Manager/Distributor Consultant for a major orthopedic device company. My younger brother is a Satellite Communications major turned Rancher (his sweet spot truly is on the back of a horse). And I'm, well, you know my story. All of us have our assignments "each according to his unique ability" (Matthew 25:15). We each have our place in God's plan for the utmost purpose of bringing glory to Him.

Like I said, I didn't always know this—or should I say, accept this? Sure, I loved singing and felt called to it. But I also thought my gift was mine and mine alone to direct and control...and benefit from. I had big plans to be famous, you see, to travel the world and take my place on stage in front of thousands of adoring fans. In fact, this is what most everyone wanted for me, or at least expected from me.

If you haven't already guessed this about me, I'm the type who more often than not needs a rubber mallet to the head in order to "get" what God wants from me. I can just picture Him wanting so badly to roll His eyes and shake His head as He over and over says, "Wake up! Get a clue, Child!" But, in the case of communicating *AT THE END OF MYSELF...I AM SINGER*, He met me in His perfect timing, in His perfect way.

I lie propped up in the adjustable, but terribly uncomfortable hospital bed. It was approximately 3:00 A.M., and I was experiencing one of my most coherent moments I had had in the five days of being heavily sedated as my body recovered from the one-hundred-mile-an-hour impact it had endured. I was in deep conversation with my two care-taking sisters. (In the sensitive hours after experiencing a near-death car accident, you don't just "chat.") I was wrestling my thoughts out loud to them: Why in the world would God spare me? Why was the life of another woman so tragically taken? I wondered: What was my purpose? What was I supposed to do with my second chance? At that moment, my body lurched in a dry-heave convulsion, a response to my empty stomach meeting the power of the meds administered through my I.V. drip. My sister Shari held the little bean-shaped spit tray in front of my mouth while I gagged, spewed scarce traces of liquid, and cringed at the immense pain in my broken ribs. She gently wiped my cracked lips and then my sweating forehead with a cool cloth. In utter exhaustion, I gingerly leaned back against the lumpy pillows and said with more certainty than I had ever experienced, "I know what it is."

In my weakest physical and emotional moment, God had met me in His unfathomable strength and directly spoke my life's unique truth: "Jackie, you *must* sing..." He didn't even have to make the rest of the message audible. I got the tagline loud and clear: "FOR ME!"

From then on, I knew my distinct call. I didn't know the "when," "where," "how," or "to what extent," but I knew the "who," the "what," and the "why." In my bones (broken though they were) I knew my gift was no longer my own to direct. I needed to get serious about how I might give it back to the Giver and disregard how it might serve me. "Each one should use whatever gift he has received to serve others, faithfully administering God's grace in its various forms. If anyone speaks, he should do it as one speaking the very words of God. If anyone serves, he should do it with the strength God provides, so that in all things God may be praised through Jesus Christ" (1 Peter 4:10-11).

Even after accepting a charge such as this, one doesn't just jump into a glorious chariot and run where the beautiful white horse leads. It takes time and much—I mean MEGA—discernment. It takes coming to the end of oneself fully and without reservation. It means living in harmony with discomfort and becoming friends with struggle. It calls for total humility and vulnerability. It means doing the hardcore emotional and spiritual work that self-reliance rejects.

Philippians 2:12-13 tells us: "Continue to work out your salvation with fear and trembling, for it is God who works in you to will and act according to His good purpose." It's a paradox of the human and divine element of our faith. We "work out" our salvation, and yet God "works" in us to accomplish it. In other words, we have to find a stewardly balance where we meet God in a co-laboring partnership, where we are active, responsible participants in our faith, but we yield to the Almighty's reign over all of it.

Some would take one look at this heed-your-call description and say, "Forget it! Too much effort! I'll take my chances living right here on the surface of life." I can relate to that comfort-zone mentality. I won't lie: Christian servanthood can be extremely burdensome. But it can also be the greatest blessing one will ever know.

After seven years of "fearing and trembling" in my ministry call, I'm still amazed at God's providence. He continually and mercifully grants me opportunity to present new ministry programs all over the nation and impact audiences in ways I never dreamed, nor could make happen on my own. He's made possible the professional recording of my music and its radio play to reach way beyond my capability. He's opened unexpected writing avenues to me as a magazine columnist and book reviewer, and now as a book author. He's reshaped the young girl who once wanted a country music career with all its glitz and glory, and turned her into an obedient (most of the time) servant who really doesn't care if anyone knows her name, but rather simply wants people to know Him through her work.

Doing my small part in God's master plan with the gifts I've been given fulfills my co-laboring charge, and in turn, fulfills my life more than I could have independently fathomed or directed. I claim wholeheartedly what Paul encourages: "Make a careful exploration of who you are and the work you have been given, and then sink yourself into that. Don't be impressed with yourself. Don't compare yourself with others. Each of you must take responsibility for doing the creative best you can with your life" (Galatians 6:4 MSG).

At the end of myself, I am Singer…and whatever else He calls me to be.

APPLICATION

Looking back, it does not surprise me that God worked so boldly in my weakest physical and emotional moment. I now look at such times of suffering in my life as a chance to rejoice in how God will work and multiply my strength and faith. I'm reminded:

> *And we rejoice in the hope of the glory of God. Not only so, but we also rejoice in our sufferings, because we know that suffering produces perseverance; perseverance, character; and character, hope. And hope does not disappoint us, because God has poured out His love into our hearts by the Holy Spirit, whom He has given us* (**Romans: 5: 2-5**).

SELF-REFLECTION

How has God met you in your individual struggles? Were you able to embrace a hope that "does not disappoint?" What perseverance, character, and hope were birthed in this process, and how has it enhanced your walk?

APPLICATION

In the sometimes excruciating process of discernment of God's will in my life, I rely on the promises in the following Bible passages:

- *Trust in the Lord with all your heart and lean not on your own understanding; in all your ways acknowledge Him, and He will make straight your paths* (**Proverbs 3:5-6**).
- *"For I know the plans I have for you," declares the Lord, " plans to prosper you and not harm you, plans to give you hope and a future. Then you will*

call upon Me and come and pray to Me, and I will listen to you. You will seek Me and find Me when you seek Me with all your heart" (**Jeremiah 29:11-13**).
- *Yet he did not waver through unbelief regarding the promise of God, but was strengthened in his faith and gave glory to God, being fully persuaded that God had power to do what He had promised* (**Romans 4:20-21**).

SELF-REFLECTION

What do you feel God is trying to communicate to you as his co-laboring partner? With what unique skills has He equipped you to serve? How might you use them to answer more fully His call on your life? What will it take for you to trust God in this way?

CHAPTER EIGHT

At the end of myself...
I AM CHILD OF GOD.

◦◦◦

I listen and watch as my daughter stands in the middle of the other Bible-school-attending three-year-olds and belts out, "We want to see (clap, clap, clap)...We want to see (clap, clap, clap)...We want to see Jesus lifted high!" The children on each side of her choose either to use their energy to sing the words, or do the actions, or look out into the audience for their Moms and Dads. But not Jenna. She's raising her hands and singing every word, all the while smiling at her teacher and beaming Mom and Dad. And she doesn't stop there. After her class is dismissed from the platform, she joins Ted and me in the pew, only to sing along and do the actions with the older classes as they take the platform one by one and present the other ten songs in the program. We hear the people behind us whisper that they can't believe she knows all of the words and actions to every song and has learned them in basically less than five hours. Ted and I are torn between the same awe and the parental obligation to keep our child quiet and politely seated in the pew. In the end, the awe wins out and we watch in disbelief and thanksgiving as our daughter unassumingly reveals her unbridled childlike faith.

Jenna's innocent approach to faith is something I earnestly work to emulate. She makes no apologies for her joy. Without question, she accepts Truth (God made the stars and the moon) and feels Love (Jesus loves me this I know). She hasn't yet come to a place where experience outweighs innocence, where the burns of life scar, where the calluses of disappointment potentially harden. Most importantly, she hasn't yet had a chance to get in the way of God's objective in her life.

The title track to my first CD is called "Raging Wildflower." It summarizes by way of the wildflower metaphor what I've included in this book: how I have raged through life, hindering God's objective by my self-reliance. The second verse and chorus read:

> *Bloomin' in my own sweet time,*
> *I fight life's meter and rhyme.*
> *Against the grain I will grow,*
> *But in open prairie I let go...*
> *I am a raging wildflower,*
> *Stung by wind and kissed by Heaven's showers,*
> *Simple, but intricately made,*
> *Staring at the horizon every day.*

Thankfully, I've come to know His unfathomable power can override all of my wildflower tendencies, as the song's last verse reveals:

> *My heart has seen the flood and flame*
> *Leaving me never quite the same.*
> *Better and stronger I now stand,*
> *Cupped in my Creator's loving hand.*
>
> —"Raging Wildflower," Jackie Quinn

In essence, I have finally come to that open prairie horizon where my wind-burned vulnerability has met the gentle but strong embrace of the sun. I have reclaimed my Child role and yielded to my Father's strength and wisdom. I have come full circle to what Mark 10:14-16 tells us: "'Let the little children come to Me, and do not hinder them, for the kingdom of God belongs to such as these. I tell you the truth, anyone who will not receive the kingdom of God like a little child will never enter it.' And He took the children in His arms, put His hands on them and blessed them."

In all the roles of my life—Daughter, Sister, Friend, Wife/Husband's Partner, Mother, Singer, Child of God—I have climbed into His arms and felt His blessed touch. From this peaceful perch, I want to continue to work out my place in each life role and do my part to fulfill my co-laboring charge, knowing what is and isn't for me to carry. I want to actively be a good steward of the opportunities given me in each of these areas, all the while yielding to the ebb and flow of balanced relationship. Most importantly, I want to continue to trust and draw nearer to Him, avoiding self-reliance pit-falls.

To some of you, hearing words like "childlike" and "yielding" may make the AT THE END OF MYSELF...I AM CHILD OF GOD concept seem more like a sign of retreat, a crawling back into the womb of sorts. Be assured, claiming this role in one's faith walk is not a sign of weakness in God's eyes. To be childlike by the world's standards is not the same as to be childlike by Heavenly standards. It takes great strength, perseverance, and maturity to be "weak" in this way...

- "Be diligent in these matters; give yourself wholly to them, so that everyone may see your progress" (1Timothy 4:15).
- "Fight the good fight of the faith. Take hold of the eternal life to which you were called" (1 Timothy 6:12).

- "I press on toward the goal to win the prize for which God has called me heavenward in Christ Jesus" (Philippians 3:14).

In my estimation, diligence, fighting, taking hold, and pressing on have nothing to do with retreat! In fact, they prove growth and confidence in the Lord.

By the grace of God, I've thankfully experienced this kind of progress. Just as a new-born calf reacts to its unfamiliar world, stumbling at first to gain its footing, then feeling comfortable enough to stand near its mother, and eventually confident enough to run and play with the other spring babies, so has been my journey. I've undergone such extensive growth—from stumbling over my denial-stricken "comfort," to understanding and embracing vulnerability in relationship, to realizing and developing my partnership with God. I've gone from hearing stories of Love in Sunday School, to learning what it is to doubt and distrust Love after being hurt deeply, to finally relenting enough to truly know and allow Love to penetrate my soul. Even in times of struggle, I now walk in confidence, knowing where I've been and where I'm headed.

> *When I'm looking in the mirror,*
> *All I see is me staring back at me,*
> *But when I'm looking in Your word,*
> *The reflection reveals You in me.*
> *At the end of myself,*
> *You are there, You are there*
> *And at the end of myself,*
> *I'm not scared, I'm not scared*
> *'Cause You are there.*

—"At the End of Myself," Jackie Quinn

At the End of Myself

I rejoice that God will continue to shape me as His child, challenging me to own my problems, confess my failures and imperfections, ask for and offer forgiveness, develop my talents, continue to seek truth and help, and most importantly, learn to love as He has loved me. I celebrate that He is truly and hugely *at the end of myself!* I pray the same for you in all the roles of your life.

APPLICATION

As a Child of God, I make Proverbs 31: 25, 30-31 my goal: *She is clothed with strength and dignity; she can laugh at the days to come....A woman who fears the Lord is to be praised. Give her the reward she has earned, and let her works bring her praise at the city gate.*

SELF-REFLECTION

Where are you in the circle of innocence and experience? Have you come full circle back to your childlike center? If so, do you find yourself refreshed and newly "clothed with strength and dignity" in a way that only Heaven can measure? Is there joy in your days to come? What God-fearing work still needs to be done to reach this maturity?

APPLICATION

In my Child of God pursuit, I long for God to delight in me. Psalm 147:10-11 tells us: *His pleasure is not in the strength of the horse, nor his delight in the legs of a man; the Lord delights in those who fear Him, who put their hope in His unfailing love.* I also long to hear Him say to me the words of Matthew 25:23: *Well done, good and faithful servant!*

SELF-REFLECTION

Have you come to the end of yourself as a Child of God? Do you feel God's delight and satisfaction? What would it take to achieve this in your walk?

WORKS CITED

Cloud, Henry, and John Townsend. <u>12 Christian Beliefs That Can Drive You Crazy: Relief from False Assumptions</u>. Grand Rapids: Zondervan, 1995.

Eldredge, John, and Stasi Eldredge. <u>Captivating: Unveiling the Mystery of a Woman's Soul</u>. Nashville: Thomas Nelson, 2005.

Hall, Mark. "Who Am I?" <u>Casting Crowns</u>. Club Zoo Music, 2003.

Lucado, Max. <u>Cure for the Common Life: Living in Your Sweet Spot</u>. Brentwood: Integrity, 2005.

- - - . <u>It's Not About Me: Rescue from the Life We Thought Would Make Us Happy</u>. Brentwood: Integrity, 2004.

Omartian, Stormie. <u>The Power of a Praying Parent</u>. Eugene: Harvest House, 1995.

ABOUT THE AUTHOR

Founder of Wildflower Ministries, Jackie Quinn is a nationally recognized Christian singer, inspirational speaker and author. She is best known for her non-denominational music programs, her *Raging Wildflower* and *Celebrate the Child* CD recordings, her *Spirit of the Plains Magazine* columns and book reviews, and her *Fill My Cup* women's events and ministry leadership seminars.

Besides working with the best in the Christian music industry on her recording projects, Jackie has shared the platform with many well-known Christian musicians as well as popular international Christian speakers and authors. In addition, she has achieved national radio play of *At the End of Myself*, the single release from her *Raging Wildflower* CD and companion song testimony to her *At the End of Myself* book.

Jackie appears nation-wide at churches, women's conferences, professional retreats, youth events, and federal and state correctional facilities. A woman of influence, Jackie has spurred thousands to a more balanced faith life and a more intimate partnership with God.

To schedule Jackie Quinn for an event, please contact:

Wildflower Ministries
515.490.9065
www.jackiequinn.com

NOTES

NOTES

NOTES

NOTES

NOTES

NOTES

NOTES

NOTES

NOTES

NOTES

NOTES

NOTES

Printed in the United States
212966BV00001B/1/A